In My Own Words

John Devereux

www.boundstonebooks.co.uk

First published in Great Britain in 2009 by Boundstone Books, Little
Boundstone, Littleham, Bideford. EX39 5HW.

Reprinted 2010 including additional material
Second reprint 2016 with further additional
material

ISBN 978-0-9568709-2-6

Edited by David Hogan

Cover photograph courtesy of Pat Haddrell

Printed and bound in Great Britain
by BookPrintingUK

www.boundstonebooks.co.uk

'In My Own Words' evolved out of times shared in front of Johnny's coal fire when his recollections were freely given and very much enjoyed. Then one day at the beginning of 2007 he asked if I would write his story. It has been a pleasure and a privilege; one he would be happy to know is now being shared by others.

Pamela Vass

Foreword

This little book contains the recollections of one man who lived through most of the 20th Century. This was a time of great change in Europe as a result of the Industrial Revolution and the subsequent migration of labour from the rural areas to the towns and cities. The Great War had scythed a swathe of death and destruction through Europe's nations and their populations in the early part of the century, dramatic events that left rural England reeling from the loss of its manhood. Many working class families still living in the countryside at the beginning of the 20th Century invariably did so under primitive and harsh conditions and it was into such a deprived environment that John Devereux was born and grew up. His story, recounted here, *"in his own words"* is a record of life as it was experienced for many people of that time and culminates in his death at 92 in 2008.

He tells of the mean and cramped living conditions that were the lot of many farm workers of that era. He speaks of the iniquitous tied cottage system that permitted landowners to control the lives of their workers. His position as the eldest in his family was soon to be severely tried when his mother became confined to an asylum and his father tragically killed in a freak accident.

When World War II came and repeated the carnage experienced in the Great War in a more sophisticated and technologically advanced manner, John finds himself a soldier. He recalls how fortune in the form of his foot-balling skills saved him from the front line but then conspired to thrust him into the jaws of danger closer to home. He reflects on his years in the Bomb Disposal Squad of the Royal Engineers and readers cannot help but be astonished at his ability to survive in an occupation where life expectancy was measured in months. His comment, "I carried me football boots to war ..." does little to communicate just how significant they were in moulding his life at that time.

With the war over, like many of his contemporaries, John struggles to make his way in civilian life but flourishes on meeting and marrying his wife, Rene. Their life, whilst hard, was happy, their stoicism, determination and hard work enabling them to build a simple, if not comfortable, home together. John tells of his working and playing life with charming candour using a unique vernacular, being the combination of Herefordshire and Devonshire dialect. Where possible this has been reflected in Pamela Vass's transcription of his words. He speaks of his work in support of the village that became his home and which he loved so dearly, Littleham in North Devonshire, England.

In conclusion, John frankly recalls the desperate times of his wife Rene's decline and subsequent death. He speaks freely of this experience and his feelings and once more the reader appreciates the rectitude that carried John through all of the other adversities that attended his life. Although not apparently ill at the time, his words that complete the final paragraph of his recollections, "The story have ended ..." were strangely prophetic, as he died not long afterward.

For those who believe they knew him, this story may still contain surprises, for those who didn't, it is a fascinating and candid reflection of a life and times slowly receding into history.

David Hogan –Editor –May 2008.

Early Times

I was born in a little place called Holmer outside Hereford on October 21st 1915. There was just my sister Lena before me. She was eighteen months older than me. Two years later came my brother Les then I had another brother called Reg – he was about another two years younger. Well, the next one was Kenny and then after him come my brother Donny about another two years later. Then Joyce was the last one in the family. That's all the little devils together. Joyce was my stepsister, the same mother.

We lived at Holmer for about four years and then we went home from school one night and found all the furniture out on the roadside. Father had lost his job and he had orders to get out of the house within a week. But he wouldn't get out so the bailiffs come along and took all his furniture, all the old bedsteads and everything and put it out on the road. I remember there was a small car waiting, a taxi I suppose. I was bundled with my sister and mother into the taxi and we went into a little cottage with my grandpa in Hereford to live for a while. I'd just started school. I was about four and a half.

Well that was where mother would send me and Lena with a basin and a penny each to a little shop across the road, where the man made soup, to get a basin full of broth. Then one day mother was ironing the clothes, it was a gas iron, before electric, and she'd iron back and forth on the table and dap the iron down and me being a nosey parker put my hand up there. And she put the iron on my hand. All the skin come off. Oh dear, we've had some games.

Well grandpa had a housekeeper and mother and the housekeeper couldn't get on very well. Any road, mother said she couldn't stick it no longer with the housekeeper. Father was working for a brewery with a steam wagon delivering beer various places but he changed his job and went to work on a farm at Hoarwithy *(Ed. on the A49 road to Ross from Hereford)* He'd got a sister living there in one of the cottages with her husband who was working for the farmer. Mother decides that's where we're going so off we goes again. She bundles up me two brothers, Les and Reg, in an old fashioned pram with long springs on each side, with me and Lena by the side. And off we set to the train at Hereford.

Any road, on the way to catch the train we met grandpa coming home from work and he said, 'Ethel,' he said, 'where do you think you'm going?'

So mother looked up to him and said, 'I can't get on with your housekeeper. We're going to Hoarwithy to stop for a while.'

Any road, we got on the train, never been on a train before in my life, frightened to death, and we got off at Ballingham station.

Illustration 1: Ballingham Station c.1910

Off comes the pram, out we get, me and Lena by the side, mother with the pram with Les and Reg in it, a mile and an half to the house. So we gets along this road and then all of sudden we come to where a lane branches off where a horse and cart have been. So mother decides that's where it is. We get a quarter of the way up, mother begins to blow a bit and says, 'my God I don't know whether I shall be able to make it or no.' Anyway, my brother gets out and me and Lena help mother push the pram up this lane to the old houses.

We had to stop with father's sister to start with because the man who worked for the farm beforehand was a good man and the farmer didn't want to put him out, so he gave him permission to stop until he found a job – perhaps a fortnight or three weeks. Then a cottage come empty, a lovely cottage belonging to this farm. Everything seemed to be going sweet. Of course we had two and a half miles from there to Dewchurch school.

Illustration 2: Dewchurch School. Built in 1865 to educate the children of poor agricultural workers and being a church school, boys and girls were strictly segregated. Now a hostelry, this restriction has been lifted. Picture courtesy of http://www.herefordshiretrail.com

On my way I had to take father's lunch out to the field where he was ploughing with the horse. That would be a lump of bread and a big lump of cheese and an onion and a bottle of tea with a sock pulled over the top of it to keep it warm.

Well then, that was all right. Time goes by and us youngsters gets hold of another young chap, I don't know what he was called, but his mother and father was better off than us and he used to go to the same school. One day on the way to school me and Lena persuades him to leave his food in a hole in the wall of an old broken down cottage and we'd have a picnic on the way home. Well of course you see, me being artful, I was first back there and I pinched his cake, sat and ate it in this old house with the sheep that used to go in there out of the way of the flies!

We were there for a little while, everything going along all right, and the farmer used to go to market on a Wednesday and he used to drink a little bit. Any road, one day father come in from the field from ploughing and the farmer was there waiting for him.

The farmer says to father, 'you haven't done enough today,' and he hit out at father whilst father was taking the gear off the horses. 'You haven't done enough work,' he said.

Father hanged up the gear on the old wooden thing at the back of the horses; he hanged it up there. And the farmer was by the door. And father went up to the farmer and hit him right out to the dung heap in the yard. So, of course, that was the end of that, we was on the road again.

Father went to see a timber hauler and he got a job with him, at a place called Paltrow. This was up another lane about a mile long where the horse and carts used to travel. I was about six or seven. Any road, how to get the furniture there? So father gets the old two-wheeled muck cart what was used for taking the manure out into the field and goes three or four times up the lane with the furniture on this cart to the new house.

(Ed. these muck carts had bodies that were articulated on the central axle enabling the load to be tipped when a catch was withdrawn. They were generally very dirty and smelly)

Oh my God, what a wonderful time we had there. It was a very good job for father, on the timber work, and I used to go down to play with the farmer's boy at the weekend. I always remember his father was a big man, a very strong man and his mother was the dearest old lady you've ever seen and she used to keep a lot of white fowls. We'd have a meal there and the old farmer would sit at table in his proper place with his trilby on, and I'd be opposite and his son on the other side and the lady in her place with her apron on. And we used to have cured bacon and egg for breakfast and the slices would be very near half an inch thick. They used to cure their own bacon see. The old boy would go out back and cut it, slice it down just like that and soon as ever he take a bite he'd put his knife and fork down on the plate and chew and chew it.

Illustration 3: Traditional two wheeled horse drawn
Muck Cart - picture courtesy of Thompson Trading

Me and Lena used to go to school at Little Dewchurch *(ed. synonymous with Dewchurch)*, and Les was just starting. I went there until I left school at thirteen. Just before I left I got a job with Mrs

Moxley and her son. My job was to deliver milk. I went there for about three weeks to live in, but that didn't suit because her was a bossy old woman. She used to play the organ at church and I used to blow the organ for her.

Illustration 4: Rarely seen these days. Manual pump organs were typical in John's younger days. The vertical device indicates the level of wind in the instrument that mustn't be allowed to fall below an indicated point. Organ pumpers were kept busy! - photo courtesy David Banga

We stopped there, at Little Dewchurch, until I was sixteen and I was working with father on old timber horses getting seven shillings a week. Well, mother decides it's too far for us to go, in the winter with the snow; sometimes it was six foot or so. We'd be home for a month at a time. And it was two mile to school for the younger ones.

Mother decides we ought to move up into the village, to try to get nearer the school.

So father got a job with another timber man called Mr Frank Bailey. And we had to move into a little two-bedroomed cottage right beside the pub at Little Dewchurch that he run with his wife and son. I always remember the toilet was up the top of the garden and of course there was no door on the toilet and I'd be sat there and someone would say, 'hello, John. All right?'

'Yes,' I'd say.

'Are you easing yourself?'

'Yes,' I'd say. What a caper! Rough and ready it was.

Illustration 5: Although typical of the outside toilet of John's younger days, this one has the luxury of a door! –picture courtesy of http://tre.ngfl.gov.uk

And Mr Frank Bailey had about fourteen big horses and timber carriages put to haul big trees out of the woods. We hadn't been there above six months when father says, 'we've got to go in to lodging, me and you.'

So I said, 'what for?'

'The boss have bought some wood down Symonds Yat, outside Monmouth,' father said. 'We've got to sleep there because he's got sleeping quarters for us, bed and breakfast and that.'

So off we go, twelve, thirteen mile, horses, timber carriage, all the gear, to this farm at the bottom of the hill at Symonds Yat.

Illustration 6: This picture of a timber carriage of John's era looks a mite optimistic. John often talked about 3 pairs of horses hauling the carriages he worked with.

And this farmer had got some old buildings and an old tumbledown cottage. This is where we was going to keep the horses but they could be turned out weekends because it was summertime. So, we were there two, three weeks when father said, 'I think we could live

8

in that cottage.' It was summertime, warm. But there was no windows, no ceiling, just an old broken down house but he said, 'I think we could manage in there, me and you. What you think about it?'

I said, 'no good me thinking about it. I can't do anything about it.'

Any road, we moved in. Father goes somewhere and buys a bed, an old bedstead; no springs but comfortable enough for us. So we moves into this old house and gets settled in. First of all we had to get a trunk from somewhere so father goes to Goodrich, towards Ross, and he goes in an old second hand place and buys this old trunk that people use for moving.

'Why is it a tin trunk?' I ask.

Father says, 'it will stop the mice and rats eating the food.'

Up till then the mice had been biting the cheese, biting the bread, but we still ate it.

So we started on our job fetching the trees down with the horses and loading it and taking it to the sawmills at Monmouth.

Well, at weekends, on a Friday night, father would set off on his pushbike and go back home and leave me there on my own to look after the horses. And in this old house there was no windows, no ceiling, no boards upstairs, just the beams – an old broken down house. So this Saturday night I decide to go to bed early. I hangs this old bag across the window, because there's no glass there, gets myself into bed, right down and comfortable, and I'm laid there more or less half asleep and all of a sudden the old bag moves to one side with somebody's hand and this woman looks in.

'Oh my God,' she says, 'there's a man in bed in there.' They was holiday people going out for a walk you see. I don't know who gave who the biggest shock!

Well father and me tottered along quietly there for a few months and then the job was over. So we pack up again and back home to Dewchurch. All the horses, father with three, me with three, but I had to follow father because he was the boss. Back home we settles in again. By this time mother had had my youngest sister, my step-sister, Joycey, she was born.

When I worked for this man with father, father head wagoner, me more or less the boy. I was getting a shilling a day for seven days a week. But it was paid straight to father in his packet. I never saw it. So I said to father, 'I'm going.'

He said, 'where do you think you'm going?'

I said, 'to get another job.'

He said, 'you can't, it's a tied cottage. If you go we shall be out of house and home again.'

So I decided to stay on, but beings as I was getting on a bit, and I wanted a pushbike and all that business, I pestered and pestered father about another job. So we decided to find something where he could work too. We got the Hereford Times but no work about, nothing about, people on the dole. So we went to see this old fella. He had a massive farm. Father told him the situation.

'Hang on a minute,' he said, 'my bailiff will be here, see what he say. He does all my business.'

Along come this chap, about forty I suppose, he looked me up and down, asked father for a reference. He got a reference, give it to him. The chap said, 'I think it'll be all right. You can start in about a fortnight's time.'

So off we go from Dewchurch to the other side of Hereford, which was about eight mile. Beautiful little cottage, two cottages up there. Lovely place. Any road there was no electric light and no water so I had to go and fetch the water from the stream down over the field, down the land, down over another field, between the ferns – taller than me – down to the brook, trickling down, filled with taddypoles. I had a jam-jar there and I took two buckets and you had to put the water in gently to get these fish out. Proper job. And I'd fetch it back up across the field to the stile then blow me down if I didn't spill half of it! So it was back down the land, over the field, between the ferns, back to the brook all over again.

Next morning, I was up at four to get the cows in. Three of us – sixty cows he had so we all had to milk about twenty.

(Ed. It is estimated that milking a 60-cow herd by hand would require 18 man hours daily. With three milkers, John would have been hand milking for 3 hours every morning and 3 hours every

evening. In between times there would be the regular daily and seasonal work to be done.)

This man had polio and was crippled up with two walking sticks but every morning about half past four he'd be up and he'd talk to they cows. He couldn't do nothing else though.

Illustration 7: Very often women were employed to do the milking (milk maids) thus releasing the men for heavier duties –picture courtesy of http://www3.shropshire-cc.gov.uk

And that morning's milk, with the nights before, had to be got to Hereford with the pony and trap by seven, with the milk in Nestle type churns. He used to stop and all these men would come and the foreman would dish it out for them to take it round the houses.

I was having thirty-seven shillings a week there.

(Ed. The milk churn was a standard size, the older galvanised iron conical, Nestle, type to which John refers held 17 gallons, weighing over 1.25cwt/64kilos! The cylindrical galvanised iron type

with the mushroom shaped lid introduced in the 1930's initially held twelve and then subsequently ten gallons – slightly less challenging for the worker to move. Each churn carried a brass plate near the top to identify the owning company and when full it would have a white paper label (either tied to the handle on the lid of the conical type and to the side handle of the cylindrical type or even pinched in the lid when it was closed), which was used for accounting purposes by the creamery or dairy.)

Illustration 8: Nestle 17 gallon (>77 litres) churn (left) with subsequent 12 (>54 litres) and 10 gallon (>45 litres) churns on right

We weren't there very long, I suppose about twelve months, before mother was took bad. By this time I was seventeen, very near eighteen and mother was took away from us; she had a nervous breakdown. She went to Berghill asylum outside Hereford. That's right, I was seventeen and my sister, Lena, who was home doing a bit of looking after us, decided to get married to a man from Brendon in Devon. He was up here because of Mrs Simmons who was master of Staghounds down in Brendon. Any road, she gave it up and came up to Wormlow and brought this man called Harry with her and that's how my sister picked him up.

Harry decided to go back to Brendon. Well of course he took my sister with him and that left the others with me and father. Any road, we couldn't carry on, looking after the baby as well, with mother in the asylum. First of all they took her to the workhouse so we had to put the three youngest ones in to the workhouse with her. But the workhouse people decided mother wasn't capable of looking after children, she was getting worse. So she was sent to Berghill asylum.

Well, we couldn't manage so father decides to move again, to go and stop with his sister. My uncle Sam was a blacksmith, got his own blacksmith's shop at Kingsthorne, Much Birch near Hereford. There was sixteen of us in the house altogether, sixteen of us in a three roomed house and one bucket lavatory across where the pigs was running to get to it. What a mess, eh?

So any road, I'm eighteen now, still plodding along quietly, didn't know the next move, until I got a job at the post office and shop just up the road at Kingsthorne with Mr Simco. He was a very nice gentleman, a retired navy man running it with his wife, and they had an old bakehouse, an old van and a man who came in with a pony and trap to deliver bread around the villages. My job was to look after the pigs, a few fowls and the garden and that and deliver telegrams to different places because there was no telephones – only to the shop.

So we bide at Kingsthorne a while. Overcrowded.

I used to go and see mother. Father and I went on a Sunday, with the push bikes, both of us, every Sunday to Berghill, which was ten mile away, on the other side of Hereford on the 'A' road – we was on the Hereford to Ross road.

Then father got a job on the threshing gear going round to different farms.

Illustration 9: Threshing machine typical of the era

And he was a man who liked his pint of beer and was never punctual to time coming home you know. Any road, we went to bed this night, all of us, and father hadn't come home from work. It got eleven o'clock, twelve o'clock, he still hadn't come home.

Aunty said, 'I don't know what's become of your father.'

Not long after a knock come on the door. Two policemen stood there. 'Mr John Devereux live here?' they said. 'I'm sorry but we've bad news,' the policeman said. 'Mr Devereux got into an accident and killed himself. Run into a telegraph pole.'

Before Father died he give his name to the people in the hospital, he had head injuries, his head was all smashed in.

It was dark at night and he had a tiny little oil lamp on his bike. The police decided the wind must have blowed his lamp out and he didn't know where he was going and he run in to a telegraph post and killed himself.

Well what be us going to do now? There was Les, Reg, Kenny, Donny, Joycey and me, the oldest, home with them; that was my family, all together. So any road the funeral come up. Who's going to pay for it? It was twenty-five pound. Father owned a pig and they had little ones, seven or eight tiny pigs, so we decided to sell they pigs to pay for it. So I got a man called Tom Day to come on a Wednesday morning to pick up the sow and the little pigs to take them to market and I think they fetched about twenty-one pound, the lot them. So my father's sister says, 'that's all right, I'll put the rest.' And we paid the bill. Father's funeral, twenty-five pound.

So that left me then, I was in charge; no mother, no father, eighteen year old. So we hung on, went on and on and that's all we could do. And I used to still go to Berghill, up to the asylum every week to see mother. She'd say, 'how's your father? How haven't he come?'

The matron said, 'when you come, don't you tell her your father's been killed until I tell you.'

So I'd say, 'he's working weekends now.' And that's how it went on for a few weeks visiting mother. Then I went up there after this time and the matron in charge called me into her office.

'Mr Devereux,' she said, 'I think your mother's been in good spirit, behaved herself this week. I think it be a good idea to break the news to her today.'

And why was it she wanted me to say it that day? If my mother been off balance she'd have gone off her head completely. As it was she took it good and wanted to know how the children were. Any road, off I go, says to Aunty Florrie, I said, 'my mum is fit to come out but I got nowhere to take her.'

'Oh,' she said, 'she could come here and live with us.'

So mother comes out, to all sixteen of us in the same house. And three women in the same house – Aunty Florrie had got a daughter what was married. Well after a few weeks mother said, 'I can't stick it much longer.' It was overcrowded and half the time we didn't know whether we was going to have a meal or no. So I was out with Tom and we come across a man who lived in Pump House on the commons.

'How are you getting on?' he said.

'It t'aint going well with mother,' I said.

'No, sure enough?' he said. 'You'll have to be careful or she'll be back where she come from. You'll have to get her out of there.' And he said, 'I got the place for you. I'm moving out of Pump House and it belongs to the farmer up other end.'

'Why's it called Pump House?' I said.

He said, 'because of the big shed going shump, shump, pumping water into the big tank at top of the field and water runs down to his big house.' Of course, there was no piped water in they days.

So I walked along this wood one day, along by the main road, to the big house, seen a bloke there. 'Good evening, Sir.'

'Don't "Sir" me,' he says, 'I'm only the gardener.'

'Is the boss here?'

I told the boss the tale – how hard up we was; what happened with father and mother and living with relations and it don't go very well. 'If I don't get her away she'll be back in the asylum,' I said.

'Oh dear, we don't want that do we?' he said.

'I saw this man who says he's going from Pump Cottage,' I said.

'Why not?' he said. 'You can have the cottage. It will cost half a crown a week with the two orchards and the cider mill and the washing place at the back, but there's no water; you'll have to fetch it from down on the main road.'

So I decided I'd take the cottage. We could just about manage with mother getting ten shillings a week pension, Les working in Hereford and me getting work where I could. Any road we took it. We fell out with aunty because she didn't want us to go but we quietened that down and got friends again.

Meantime I was still working up at the shop.

'I'm sorry John', he *(ed. the postmaster)* said to me one day, 'but I'm selling up, retiring. I've sold the business and they don't want nobody to work on the garden.'

So I was pushed out of a job. By this time I'm twenty, perhaps twenty-one. I decided to try Rotherwas factory on the old Macey road. It was a big ammunitions factory where they was getting set for war, making bombs and that. Any road, I got the job, and many more my age; there were hundreds working there. So I bided there for a while and then they was building a camp outside Hereford and I got transferred there, a lot of us did.

Any road, it went all right and this job come to an end. And then I got transferred from there, waiting to go into the war you see, to the aerodrome at Credenhill. Now this is another four mile to go and I had to be there seven in the morning till seven at night seven days at week. Ten mile each way on a pushbike. Well, there I was more or less in charge of making the concrete runways for the planes – putting the shuttering up.

My mate said one day, 'what's that chap doing writing something down?'

Most of the men working there had had their papers and was waiting to be called up. Well along he comes to me.

'Good afternoon,' he says.

'Good afternoon,' I say.

'What's your age?'

'Coming twenty-four.'

'Have you had your calling up papers yet?'

'I'm waiting to be called in,' I said.

'Well we're the Royal Engineers. Would you like to join the Royal Engineers?'

I said, 'yes, why not.'

So he said, 'if you get your calling up papers within a week, forget about it because it'll be another four or five weeks till we get settled up.'

So till then I went home, waiting for the time to pass.

War-time

Illustration 10: Lance Corporal Devereux J.R. Was this before he lost the stripe or after – is it evident on his sleeve?

One day mother says to me, 'you've got to go.'
   I says to mother, 'where be I off to?'
   'Chatham Barracks,' she said.
   'Where's that?' I said.
   'Up by London.'

Well I never been there. 'Course I was like a bloody dope. I'd never been on a train or anything, living in the country. Any road, got me little case, got my football boots and a few things, and I catch the train at Hereford station coming down from Birmingham. I've still got the little case at home that I carried me football boots to war in. A little brown case.

Illustration 11: The little brown case John carried his football boots to war in.

Any road the train pulls in. I open the door and sits in the carriage, not knowing whether it's going to go back or forward.

Then this chap says to me, 'where be you off to?'

'Chatham Barracks,' I says.

'Oh,' he says, 'same as us lot. What be you called?'

'Jack, Jack Devereux.'

'Where do you live?'

'Pump House, Kingsthorne. What be you called?'

'George Emin.'

'Where be you from?'

'West Bromwich.'

So, we tiddles along, gets to Chatham Barracks. Nobody didn't know who us was or what us wanted, and they put us in a kind of a marching place in the street and marched us up to the houses. There was women waiting on the doorsteps.

'I want them,' one would call. 'I'll take four,' another would say. This woman came up. 'I want two.'

So me and my mate went into this house next door to the pub – not bad only it was on condition that we were back indoors by eight. We weren't allowed out after eight. Out next morning after breakfast we were back in the street and marched down to the barracks. They didn't know nothing about us so us played about like kids. No rifle, no uniform to put on. And we was raw; my God we was raw. One night, soon after us got into barracks, we saw this man in a uniform. Well, we didn't know who was an officer and who wasn't so us saluted him – and he was the lamplighter! He had a cap so we thought he was an officer and saluted him! Us didn't know no different.

Illustration 12: These small concrete pillboxes are the remains of a World War II 'stop-line' hurriedly constructed after the evacuation from Dunkirk in June 1940. Picture courtesy BBC

Any road, they decided we'd got to go to work in Kent on the coast, building concrete pillars with slits so they could put the rifles out to shoot out to sea. Well that was all right. All our mob, all of us twenty-two, twenty-three or twenty-four, was supposed to go to Dunkirk to make roads but in the end by the time we got called up the lads had been pushed out so we never went.

(Ed. 'the lads' – the British Expeditionary Force, although a powerful army, it was no match for the German blitzkrieg and had withdrawn, along with remnants of the French army, to Dunkirk where they were famously recovered by the 'small ships' in May 1940)

So we stayed working in Kent on the shoot out places in the banks, the pillboxes.

Whilst us was working there, still sleeping in these billets, I was took bad with quinsy in the throat, had to go into hospital for a week or more. After I come out, I reported to the barracks but nobody didn't know who I was and nobody didn't seem to want to know!

'Your unit was in civilian barracks,' this officer said, 'but we don't know where they'm gone.'

So I'm perched in Chatham barracks for another week sleeping on the floor in between beds. Bide there for about a week. Report back to the office.

'Yes, we've found your mob and they've gone to Launceston in Cornwall, under canvas in a big estate at the top of the hill. We'll give you a pass and you've to make your way down to Cornwall.'

And I thought to myself, where's Cornwall? I don't know where Cornwall is and I've no money; they hadn't even given me a pay book. Any road, the time comes.

'You've got to go join your mob. You've got to go to Paddington station.'

'Paddington station? My, that's a busy place,' I say.

Anyway, I'm standing there at four in the afternoon, and there's two redcaps belonging to the army patrolling. I told them the situation, said I got no money, just a pass to go to Launceston. 'Am I all right for Launceston?'

'No,' he says, 'the train's gone, and that's the last one for today.'

What to do? Any road, I sleeps under Big Ben in a hostel place with a lot of people, by the side of a bloke, a Scottish bloke. He asked what happened to me. He said I was lucky, not to go.

'I was one of those got away out of Dunkirk,' he said. 'Terrible it was. But tomorrow morning they won't see no more of me. They don't know I come back so I'm off.' Nerve-racking time he'd had of it. Men trying to climb on the side of the boats as they was sailing from there and they'd hang on and hang on until they fell off away out to sea. They was scrabbling to get on the small sailing boats but they were overloaded you see. Lot of them got drowned, never made it. Terrible job that was. He said you'd feel sorry, seeing all the blokes trying to get on but they couldn't because it was so overloaded. All youngsters about twenty-three, twenty-four. All youngsters. Terrible time. Terrible time.

Any road, I had to sleep there the night. Next morning I gets on the station again. I see these chaps at this army office and I tell them I've got no pay book and they let me have fifty shillings. Back on the station all these people are lining up and I says to myself, 'where the devil be I going?' I didn't even know which way the train was coming in! I had a good mind to go home.

Then all of a sudden there's these two little boys, ten to about eight, and this lady says, 'you've been down a good many time to Launceston,' – by God my ears pricked up –'so you know you have to change at Exeter.'

They was evacuees see, going down. My God, I thought, I'm not going to let they out of my sight. They boys knew exactly what to do at Exeter and I followed they. I'm a soldier about to fight for my country and I let two little boys lead me around! Any road, I get to Launceston, say goodbye to these boys and says to the station master, 'you got some army people moved in a week ago.'

'Yes,' he says, 'they'm up the hill under canvas on the estate. Lot of them. Right at the top of the hill there's double gates to the big house,' he said.

'Well,' I said, 'I'm meant to be one of them.' So I said, 'thank you very much sir,' and off I goes up the hill, up over the steep hill, get to the top, big gates, lions on the top. Then all of a sudden George Emin walks up –my friend.

'Hello, Jack, where you been? We thought you'd been posted.'

'No,' I said, 'I've been bad.'

We were there about a week, under canvas in the wood. We'd carry our cans out to a table in the field with one piece of bread and some beans on it. We were there one night, about eleven o'clock, in the dark when there's a whistle – everybody out, full kit, you're on the move. Everybody packs up, tents down and about two hundred and fifty of us march all the way down the hill back to Launceston station. All dark, no lights about, then it comes over the loudspeaker, no soldier or anybody to leave the train nowhere. We puffed along the road, got up to Exeter station. And there was girls belonging to the army with cans of tea and a sandwich for us – we wasn't allowed to get out of the train see.

Off we puffs, after a while, two or three o'clock, early morning, all dark, arrives in Paddington station up in London. There were some army lorries waiting for us. All the bombs was flashing, very near frightened us to death, never seen anything like it before, we was all raw recruits. Lorries waiting for us, moved us into Twyford Avenue between Ealing and Acton. That was civilian billets again but they was empty houses. Well, we got settled in there. Next job was fitting us up with some clothes. No rifle. They hadn't got no rifles to give us.

So we went on bomb disposal, digging up delayed action bombs all over the place. Arsenal football ground, up the Mall up in London, digging up bombs. One bomb up London was five hundred pound in weight and he was in the main sewer and the main sewer was one you could walk up and down in. Anyway we got down to this bomb, digging by hand, then the next morning he'd moved, with all the swill coming down, and you'd dig down again. We was there three or four weeks but we got him out.

Then we was back up in London, up in the streets with all the bombing going on. We'd go out at night to have a drink in Acton and wheeeee... they'd whistle, the bombs you see. You didn't know whether they were going to drop on you or not. I'd feel sorry for the old ladies – going out with blankets under their arms at three in the afternoon. They had to go early because there wasn't room in the shelters.

They had it hard up there. So any road, two and a half years I was in bomb disposal; very lucky man to get away with it. We'd go out in gangs in the morning and come back at night and say, 'where's so and so?' Not there you see. Accident. He'd got blowed up hadn't he. I remember one day we was down Shepherd's Bush in a building site, new houses, perhaps thirty or forty houses, digging up a bomb till about four o'clock. We pack up and go back to billets. Next morning we go back and we couldn't believe our eyes. There wasn't a house standing! A land mine bomb had gone down and when they bombs hit the ground they explode and expand all the way – they wouldn't go down in the soil – a couple of hundred yards away they'd knock anything flat. Some civilians were dead, some got away. I walked in and talked to this man and he never answered. The blast had taken all his breath away and he was dead.

Illustration 13: Typical activities of the Bomb Disposal squads in the early 1940's. Picture courtesy of Lt Col E.E. Wakeling ERD

After that, we went back to Twyford Avenue, to the houses they'd cleared people out of so that the army could get in – private houses with the gas works behind. That's what *he* was after *(Ed. the enemy)*, bombing the gas works. But you didn't see the danger. I've stood on the doorway at night-time watching them – our planes chasing the German planes. 'Course Michael Alvis (*Ed. from Littleham, North Devon – eventually to be John's home)* was up in they bombers risking his life for the sake of us. One night the bombs was falling heavily and we watched the planes fighting each other between the clouds. And next morning we found out that a girl had stood on the front door step, next door it was, with all the doors open, and this bomb came down and the blast killed her outright.

Any road, our time was up and we was moved on to Instow camp, by the cricket field at Instow in North Devon. I was in the football team then and I went to look at orders one night and saw I was sorted out to go, we was posted abroad. We didn't know where we was going, they didn't tell you. Went on parade the next morning and the old Sergeant Major was mad on football and he said, 'I know there's war on but you boys that's on the football team, you're not going.'

So there I was, still at Instow, experimenting on ammunitions, and from there, after about three months, our mob was moving on again. And being as I was in the football team, I got pulled out again! So I never went abroad did I, all because of my football boots.

Not long after, me and five more was moved to the top camp at Westward Ho! Our job there was experimenting on different things. The first job was to put a Bailey bridge over the pebble ridge at Westward Ho! That was to save the tanks going along the road – they could get over the pebble ridge onto the beach.

Our next job was to plant these dead mines in a field that was marked out on the beach. Then the tide would bring the sand in to about three foot and cover them over. The next time we'd go there we'd find them showing, the sand would be gone back again. Now this was all done to find out what time we could attack the Germans.

We could go on a certain tide and could drive tanks off and the mines wouldn't go off because they was covered with sand. But you mustn't go on the next tide because they'd be showing and that was the danger. That was one job. Two hundred and fifty delayed action bombs we set.

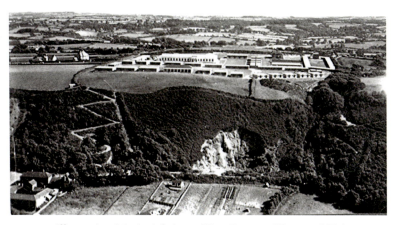

Illustration 14: Aerial view of Top Camp at Westward Ho!

Illustration 15: Holidaymakers in the courtyard at Top Camp in 1939, shortly before it was taken over by the army.

Our next job was to build bridges on Westward Ho! old cricket field. These bridges were built with wire – big wires. It was a job to be done quick over little rivers and on these wires, which would be about seven or eight of them, from one place to another. There was a mesh wire built over them so the lorries could get across the river. We spent a lot of time on that job, then after that we were back experimenting with mines. We'd go to Appledore, take out ammunition and then go by boat to Crow point near Braunton to experiment with the mines – live ones this time. We put them in the sand hills with a wire going up the beach to set them off, blowing up the sand hills. That was done to see what kind of ammunition they had to use when they got abroad to blow up different places.

Where did we go from there? Well, we done that for at least six months at a time. And then we'd go back to Westward Ho! again to experiment on how long it would take to build a Bailey bridge – put him up and pull him down, see how quick we could do it. And this was all done when you went abroad getting over different rivers, to see how quick you could do it for the troops to cross. Master job.

Then they would take us right out to sea on an old raft towing behind. And that was done to see what they could use in case they got pushed out abroad again. To see how quick they could get away.

I was stationed at Chepstow for five weeks while I was at Westward Ho! The order came, five men to go to Chepstow and I was one of them – very near going back home. There was a horse artillery place at Chepstow and we were there building these round huts for them. So one Sunday I said to my mate, 'I'd like to go home to Hereford.'

'Us'll go after church,' he said.

So after church us set off. We was going to do something wonderful. Us would catch a lift and we'd be home. Well us had to walk damn near all the way! Us had a little lift just before we got to Monmouth but nobody would pick us up you know, not two soldiers. Anyway, I gets home to Kingsthorne just in time to have my tea, then I had to go back to Hereford, six miles, to get the train back. Thirty miles in total we'd walked.

So any road we altered that caper. The next Sunday my mate said, 'we'll take the truck. I'll make sure there's plenty of petrol in it.' We'd have got locked up if they'd found out. We went home most weekends after that until we was back at Westward Ho!

We was in wooden chalets at the barracks at top camp. Two of us in each one in bunk beds. I was in the bottom, George Emin up top. It was a holiday camp, hundreds of wooden chalets, and the army took it over.

Illustration 16: The chalets John was billeted in.

There was a big swimming pool in there as well. After the war it went back to the owners and carried on as a holiday camp again. To eat you went over to the big house. I'd take me mess tin and get my grub. Good food it was. Plenty of it. There used to be a big dance hall over there too.

We'd be on parade every morning after breakfast. Everything all polished up – boots, weapon, everything. The old bugle would go and out you'd be. Then Saturday and Sunday you'd go on a march. We didn't have no ammunition though, unless you was doing two hours guard duty on the gate. But even then you'd have the bayonet fixed and the orders were to stab, not shoot, if you got into trouble. But we never had any trouble at Westward Ho! Not with the Germans anyhow.

I come across German blokes as prisoners of war. They was lovely chaps. When they was took prisoner they put them out on jobs and sometimes two or three would be in your gang. They would say, 'we didn't want the war.' They was the same as us. Made to go to war. It wasn't the ordinary German people what wanted the war. They was happy to work alongside us – they was treated the same as us. They had them at Monkleigh working on the farms, living on the farms. They was trusted. Lots of them stayed if they picked up a maid. I suppose the same thing happened out there.

The worse was if you got captured by the Japanese. They was really cruel to our people. We had a bloke driving in Mitchells and he was captured and spent three and a half years as a prisoner of war. You never knew, he said when they was going to pick up a gun and shoot you. It was terrible hard.

I was lucky. I had no trouble. Mind, there was one bloke who used to throw his weight about a bit out on the jobs at Westward Ho! One day we was on the slipway and he thought he was going to have a bit of a game with me so I upped and gave him one. I hit him, bang on the chin, rolled him down the hill. I used to do a bit of boxing see. My brother was a good boxer. I used to go Hereford with him. We had an old washhouse out the back of the house and we had a punch bag in the middle. I'd go out there punching at him, exercising see.

Any road, an officer come on the scene, wanted to know what happened. They took a stripe off me so I had to work hard to get it back. *(Ed. John had become a Lance Corporal by this time.)* I had witnesses to say this bloke was always throwing his weight about and I happened to lose my temper and hit him. I got off light really. There were over 1,000 troops there and I boxed against other units. Sometimes you'd get a hiding. A bloke hit me right out once. You'd wake up the next morning feeling sore for yourself!

One way and another, I spent three years at Westward Ho! and then the war was over and we was waiting to be de-mobbed. I was still with my friend, George Emins. He was from West Brom, Birmingham, and we'd been together through all that I have told you. All of it. He was a Territorial *(ed. Territorial Army)* man before the war so he got his passing out papers before me while we was still at Westward Ho! I think he was number fourteen, and I was number twenty-two.

Just then, I was due to go on leave to Hereford. George said to me, 'I shan't be here when you come back, boy, I shall be gone, demobbed.' Then he said, 'do you know, I've got to go to Hereford to get my passing out suit.'

So we shook hands to say goodbye to each other and off I went on leave. And on the Wednesday morning, I decided to go to town. I was walking through the High Street by the Buttermarket in Hereford, going down towards the bus station, which was on the way to the train station, and this army lorry passed me and sure enough, in the back of this lorry was my friend George Emin. He'd been and had his suit fitted and he was off home to West Brom.

He shouted to me, 'Devereux, come on down to the station.' So off I potters down to the station. We had about half an hour to wait for the train so we had a drink or two together. And with all the excitement of me meeting him again and him going to civvy street, we never took each other's address or phone number and I've never seen that man from that day to this. A friend of mine, Joan Swindler, tried to trace him and there were several people called that name up there but they could never find him. Nobody didn't seem to know anything about him.

We had good times together. Good times but very dangerous on times. My brother next to me, Les, got killed in the war. He got killed at the age of twenty-two. Then my brother, Reg, he'd been to the races with his mates and coming back, a police ambulance drove into them and killed three out of four on their motorbikes. Two of my brothers gone, along with father.

Well, I finished my leave and I had to go back to camp and it wasn't very long before my number come up. Well off I goes and I was demobbed and had to get my suit at Taunton instead of Hereford. They suit you out, you have a ticket to say you was de-mobbed and that was it. Strange feeling. I'd been in the army seven years, 1939 to 1946, then it come to an end. I walked out with my identity card and a pass to Hereford and that's it. Just walked out of it. Sometimes I think I made a mistake and sometimes I think I didn't.

Our commanding officer was a man called Mr Owen, Lieutenant Owen. That same man I met years later, years and years later down at Weare Giffard when we was down there to a little rally, and he was a retired Colonel by then. Anyway, Lt. Owen was at Westward Ho! down at Torridge House and when you got de-mobbed you had to go down the day before to see him. His job was to try and persuade you to carry on and make a career of it. They offered to make me a Sergeant straight away. I was a Corporal see. He said, 'you won't know what civvy street is like, it'll be hard for you.' But I didn't take no notice. A lot carried on but I'd had enough.

So there it was, Jonathan, you had your marching orders.

Illustration 17: Private Devereux J.R. Picture from John's effects.

Littleham Times

So off I goes, back home to mother in the little cottage called Pump House on the Common at Kingsthorne. But before that I'd already picked up this lovely girl of mine, called Irene.

Illustration 18: Lance Corporal Devereux (his stripe now restored) with Rene –picture from John's effects

We were married for fifty-two years but I knew her for fifty-four, fifty-five really. And she lived with her retired father – he was an invalid, gassed in the first war – in Montague Place at Clovelly Road in Bideford; number eight it was.

Well, I went home to Hereford and got a job with a timber hauling firm and the boss was a man called Wilf Morgan. Any road, he had an old lorry and I used to go to the woods and pick up pea sticks, kidney sticks, clothes props, posts and everything; load it up and we'd drive into Hereford and I would sit on the back of the lorry shouting, 'kidney bean sticks, pea sticks,' everything. And the people could come out and have them. And that was my daily job.

Anyway, that came to an end. In the meantime Rene had said, 'I won't see you again when you go back to Hereford.'

I said, 'I'll be back maid,' – and there was this phone box and I used to wait there for it to ring, still phoning very near every day. And then I couldn't get a job in Hereford at the time so I decided to mother that I'd go back to Devon. So I packed up a little case of belongings, walked up the top of the common and mother waved me goodbye. I'm off to Devon again to be with Rene. We went to live with her father – she'd lost her mother – at eight Montague Place.

From there I got a job at Bailey Bartlett *(Ed. Builder's Merchant)* at East the Water, on the saw bench. And the boss there was a man called Mr Grant, Charlie Grant. And I couldn't get on very well with him so after a while I left there and I went to work at the laundry at Westward Ho! So any road, Rene was working for a Mr Hayward at Devon Creameries, in the shop. Well after a while I left the laundry and her boss, Mr Hayward, come to see me. He wanted a van driver. So I took the job, at six pound ten a week.

So the time goes on, we decide to get married. She was a chapel woman, so we married at the old chapel that used to be in Bridge Street in Bideford *(Ed. Now demolished)*. So that was all right, everything went well.

Illustration 19: John and Rene's wedding – picture from John's effects

Then we decided to buy the little house that she was living in. And we bought number eight Montague Place for six hundred pound. We bide there for a while and by this time it's coming summertime and I was outside leaning against the window and some people moved into number twelve. And the old gentleman was in a wheelchair, crippled up with arthritis.

'Hello, sir,' I said.

'I'm really a local man,' he said, 'but I've been away working. I worked for Clovelly estate in the sawmills, years ago but I've got arthritis now.'

In the meantime, this was about 1947, I broke my leg at High Bickington playing football and I was in plaster for six months. So any road I got friendly with this old fella, Jim Jewel he was called, and after a while we decided I could get along clutching his wheelchair without my crutch and we'd sit on Clovelly road watching the traffic go up and down.

Every week I'd go to the hospital. I always took me slippers just in case they took the plaster off. So this morning, Rene said, 'you've got to go to the hospital.'

I said, 'yes, but I'm not taking my slippers, I carried they damn things back and forward and the doctor hadn't taken it off.'

Any road, this day he said, 'I think I'll take it off.'

I said, 'you can't.'

He said, 'why not?'

I said, 'because I hadn't got my slippers.' Any road, he took it off anyway.

So I was still friendly with this dear old gentleman called Mr Jewel when the time come that I had to pack up football – I were thirty-six year old then. Seven years I'd been in Meddon Street and all that time I went there to play cards with him at night. He said to me one day, he said, 'John, I'm getting worse.' His wife's sister was stopping and she died, then his wife died and both were buried at Clovelly. So any road, he had to have a housekeeper, very nice lady and she looked after him well. Now he had a sister that lived down Meddon Street, right opposite the almshouses but she never used to come up and see him nor nothing. He said to me one day, he said, 'all the gear I got out the back, take it away, it's yours.'

I said, 'I'm sorry,' I said, 'I can't do it, I can't take anything away from this house while you'm living.'

'Well,' he said, 'it's yours.'

So in the end he had to go in the Torridge hospital and he promised me all this and he promised me all that. Any road, the time come he died. And before he died he said to me, 'John, I think the house should be yours.'

Of course that was no good by word of mouth but he never lived long enough to have it altered. He died and sure enough he was buried at Clovelly. After the funeral his sister was there and being she was the only one close to him she had everything. And sad to say, I come away empty-handed. And my pockets is still empty today.

I got friendly with Mr Jewel's brother and he had a big farm at Woolsery. Brother-in-law it was and he said to me one day, he said, 'John what be you'm going to do with the house.'

I said, 'what do you mean?'

He said, 'it's yours isn't it?'

I said, 'no, it's gone to his sister.'

And he was very upset about it. He said, 'for all that you've done.'

Illustration 20: John with Rene and their friend, Joan. Picture from John's effects

I used to hire a car – I never had one in they days – I'd hire a car and take Mr Jewel to Newquay and places like that and pay for it myself. But it's a funny thing. You sit back and think, for all the good health I've had, I've been paid over and over for all the things I've done for people.

So any road, we carried on.

Rene said, 'I'd like to go out on the main road to live and there's a house going, thirty-four, opposite Madge's garages in Clovelly Road.'

So we went to see the house, very nice place, and we decided we'd buy it. So I see Mr Percy Cox, he was to do with the building society, the Bristol & West, and he bought the place for us. So any road we moved from number eight to number thirty-four and we moved in there right opposite the garage. Rene used to work in the shop and I used to drive the van.

And we bide there for several years, things going very well, contented... until I got friendly with Edgar Brend. Mr Edgar Brend lived at Littleham in the council houses. So after a while we got more friendly, we used to go out there to tea on a Sunday, and Rene said to him one day, 'I'd like to come here to live.'

Mrs Brend had a big family all growed up living in Langdon so we took the bottom part of the house there. Very happy, very nice, but my wife couldn't get on with them. So it was back to Bideford, to Lime Grove this time. So we bide there three or four years and Edgar Brend said, 'I believe there's a little old cottage going up in the village.'

I said to him, 'who does it belong to?'

And he said, 'Mr Stevens the farmer. He got two cottages. One is number seven and the other is number nine but,' he said, 'the man as is living in number seven is leaving the farmer and that one will be empty. But he already promised the man in number nine number seven if he wanted it because nine is an old broken down house and number seven is done up nice.'

So after a week I went to see him and he said, 'Frankie is going out and the people at number nine is moving into number seven and you can have number nine.'

So I took it. Well the house wanted a lot doing to. So I went to see the farmer again.

'You can have it,' he said, 'but I'm not spending no money on it.'

Well, we decided to take the house. My God it needed a lot doing to it. So me and Rene set about it, to do the house up. And when I told them the tale, Tony Brend and his girlfriend and another man called Keith Phelps and his wife, who lived down the road in a little galvanised bungalow, came to help. We was there a couple of months doing it up and none of them charged me a halfpenny.

Any road, it come to the time it was getting towards the end and it was on a Sunday night and it was snowing hard and we'd been there working until about ten o'clock. But we was still living in Bideford at the time so off we sets in an old Ford car, me and Rene to go home and the snow was coming down hard. And we gets half way down wagon road and the snow was coming down so hard that the old wipers wouldn't get the snow off the screen so I had to jump out and get it off. And I gets back in the car and I says to Rene, 'that's it, I'm not doing any more to the old house, I'm not going there.'

Any road, just before we left that night Tony Brend said to me, 'are you going to Bristol tomorrow?'

'Yes,' I said, 'I am.' I was on the road working for North Devon Farmers.

'Can you call at Taunton,' he said, 'at some shop and get two half-inch paint brushes?'

Next morning, off I starts, way to Bristol. By this time I was in a better mood. On the bypass at Taunton there was a shop what sells all these things. So I called in this shop and bought these paintbrushes and put them in the bottom of the bag I carry my food in. I gets home, living in Lime Grove then, I had me tea, settled down.

Rene said, 'I'll pack up your food for tomorrow.'

All right. Nothing was mentioned about the paintbrushes you see. So after her took out the flask – in the bottom of the bag was these two paintbrushes.

'Oh dear,' her said. 'You've altered your mind them, you'm going to carry on.'

'Yes, I am,' I said. 'I'm in a better mood.'

So after we'd had our tea, we picks the paintbrushes up, off to Littleham again. We had to paint all the windows inside. Tony Brend done the kitchen out for us; he hard-boarded all the walls all the way round. And he put a new ceiling in the kitchen, which took another week or a fortnight. But at last, everything done. Ready to move in.

Well one day, sat down having our tea. Rene said, 'I'm not going out there.'

I said, 'why not?'

'No,' she said. 'I'm used to a flush toilet and a bathroom and,' she said, 'it's not out there. The only thing that's out there is a bucket toilet top of the garden. I'm not going to that.'

So I'm back to see the farmer again about having the sewer put in. No, he's not going to pay any money on it. Well, I decided to do it myself. So I went to see the surveyor, told him all about it.

He said, 'yes, you get all the digging done, get the manhole built and I'll come out and inspect it.'

So I had a week's holiday and I dug from the main sewer right up through the old shed, put the pipes in, made the manhole and sent for him again.

He come out and had a look at it. 'Are you a lorry driver?' he said.

I said, 'yes sir.'

'Well,' he said, 'the way you've done this job,' he said, 'you should be a builder.' And he passed it out. All finished.

Then I said to him, 'well, this big shed is no good as it is. Could I turn it into a garage?'

'Yes,' he said, 'but you'll have to put a concrete floor in and a concrete drive up to it from the road.'

So I did that job as well after we moved in [*ed: 1963*]. Rene was very pleased. So it went on and she wanted some more jobs done, wants a fence put up between the gardens. See the farmer again.

'No, John,' he said. 'I told you when you went there, it's cheap rent; I'm not spending anything on it.'

So I've done jobs all the time I lived there, I never went to see him no more.

Illustration 21: John's cottage in Mount Pleasant, Littleham, (far right) recently restored and named Devereux's.

I was still working at the time for North Devon Farmers, travelling to Bristol two or three times a week. Four or five in the morning I'd set out, sometimes get home eight or nine at night. I was there for thirteen years and then there was about ten of us made redundant. I was looking for another job and a man called Alan Marshall, which was a great friend of mine, now passed away, found me a job at Orleigh Mill.

I'd been at Orleigh Mill about a fortnight and my mother died in Hereford. So I went to see Mr Dick Sanders and explained everything to him. Mr Sanders was a real gentleman.

He said to me, 'John,' he said, 'you go, go home to see to everything.'

So off I goes, home to Hereford, back to the old Pump House at Kingsthorne. Seen to mother's funeral. Everything went very smooth until my brother Kenny stepped in. Now he was a chap that had spent a lot of life home with mother and mother had spent most of her money on him, different things.

He said to me after the funeral, he said, 'I'm having this and I'm having that and I'm having something else.'

Being as I was the oldest son I was entitled to everything but I wouldn't have it that way. I said to him, 'you get nothing, you've had your share.' And I said, 'everything goes to Lena,' my sister which was older than me, because she'd looked after mother for the last two or three years, and I think she deserved it. And the only thing I had from that house was a little old fashioned wireless that I've got upstairs today.

Sometime after, Kenny died, of asthma, he couldn't breathe.

After settling up I returned to my present home where I am now, to my wife Rene. I went to see Mr Sanders. I said, 'I'm sorry I've been away.'

And he said, 'that's all right, John.' And he paid me my wage for the time I'd been away.

At the time I was still looking for another job, because his wasn't a regular job. I wanted a job lorry driving. So Alan Marshall came to me again.

'I hear you're looking for a driving job,' he said.

I said, 'yes, I am.'

He said, 'there's a job going with Rawle Gammon and Baker but,' he said, 'you'll have to wait a while until this other man leaves.'

After a while, I got a job with Rawle, Gammon and Baker driving all over North Devon. Mostly over Hartland to different building firms. All the way down to Launceston, all over the place.

In the meantime, the house that I live in today used to belong to a Mr Stevens down the farm. And if I got home at five o'clock I used to go down and help him on the farm a bit. And I helped him, I suppose, for about fifteen years. And I never got one penny off that man for what I done, not one penny. Then he was took bad and he died. And his brother, Arthur, that lived in Abbotsham Road, where the big school is now, come to me and asked if I'd look after his sheep. So I looked after his sheep whilst they was lambing. And I used to get up at five in the morning and make sure they was lambing all right, give them a bit of feed, come home and have my breakfast, off to work, come home at night, go down to see them again.

Well in the end the farmer died, in a little bungalow at Northam, and the bank people come to me and they wanted to know if Mrs Stevens had made any arrangements. And I said 'I don't know what's going on.' But any road, the small rent that I was paying I had to pay to Mrs Stevens at Northam now.

So any road, the years passed by and my wife Rene was working at the school in Abbotsham road. She was there for twenty-four years as a cook.

She said to me one day, 'John,' she said, 'I feel I can't go on much longer.'

Rene had a friend called Valerie Bond that lived at Monkleigh. Now my wife was going in to work on the bus which used to pass the door. But the bus firm decided they wan't going to come up the village any more, they was only going through the bottom end, and this lady, which was a great friend of me and Rene, she used to go from Monkleigh every afternoon in her car, go to Bideford and pick Rene up and drop her off at the door. And she did that four or five years, never missed.

Well time went on. My wife was took bad with cancer in her breast. She had to go to Barnstaple hospital to have her breast took off; she'd retired from her job by then. I used to go to Barnstaple after I left work every night for a fortnight and then they let her come home.

After a couple of months she had a lump come on her leg. So we went to see Dr Ford.

'I'll arrange for you to go to Barnstaple hospital again,' he said.

In the meantime she went to see a specialist up there and he confirmed it was cancer again. As if that wasn't enough she was troubled with her water. So she had to go to Barnstaple again and have her gall bladder took out. Well this lump on her leg, it was operated on, and the nurse used to come every day to dress it. And the nurse wasn't satisfied with it.

'You'll have to see Dr Ford again,' she said.

So off to see Dr Ford again.

He said, 'I think I'll send you back to Barnstaple to see the specialist.'

So off to Barnstaple we go and sure enough, they hadn't took enough of the cancer off and she had to have another operation on her leg.

Illustration 22: John and Rene later in life –picture from John's effects

Through all these years I took on some jobs about the village. I looked after the village hall, where my job was to clean all the inside, clean the windows, and cut all the grass. I used to go to bingo at the village hall pretty regular then on a Tuesday night every fortnight. Me and Richard Heddon would go up on a Tuesday morning and get it all ready for the bingo. Mr Mills from down the farm sold a piece of ground to extend the car park and we paid him a hundred pound for it. The next thing was, who was going to put up the fence between his cows and the car park? So one Saturday morning me and Mr Tony Brend – he was working at Bartletts at the time – decide that we would put up the fence, free of charge.

All my spare time I used to go down to the farm and help Mr Stevens, shovelling potatoes. And at that time he was doing about four hundred ton and I would be doing the shovelling. With Alan Smale. Well, job finished.

After a few weeks I was just moping about and I went up through the village one day, Lionel Badcock come to me. 'Just the man I want to see,' he said. 'What be you about?'

I said, 'nothing.'

'Well,' he said, 'we can't keep a young man like you idle, I can find you a job.'

'Oh, what's that?' I said.

He said, 'all the rails down the chapel, down the front of the chapel and the gates, all want re-painting, and they got to be cleaned off first. Will you do it?'

So I decide I'd go home, see my wife and tell her all about it.

Her said to me, 'John, I think you should steady up, at your age,' her said, 'you should go down a gear.'

I said, 'I'm very sorry, dear, I'm in bottom gear now, I can't go no lower.'

'Oh,' her said, 'well, you please yourself.'

I saw Lionel, took the job. I went down there, very early mornings, I didn't work all day. I was there two or three days, job done.

And I played skittles with Lionel for Littleham for about thirty-five years.

Illustration 23: Littleham 'B' skittles team circa 1970. left to right: –Keith Phelps, Lionel Badcock, Geoff Pickard, John Palmer (Captain –holding cup), Tony Brend, John Devereux, Walter Withecombe –picture from John's effects

I always helped at the village hall fetes. I haven't missed one since I've been here, forty-three years. My job mostly is to look after the big gate, to keep opening him to let the tractors and that in; a job I appreciate because I meet so many people I know

After a while I decided to sell draw tickets for the fete. I would start off around the houses; used to meet a lot of people, good friends, very nice people. And June Brend was selling too, only her had people that her could put her books out too *(Ed. sell books on her behalf)*. I always sold all my books myself, and she would beat me. So this last year I decided to go and see Dougie Hamilton, and I knowed it was coming up time to have the books and I said to him, 'have you got they books?'

And he said, 'no, not yet.'

I said, 'as soon as you get they books you bring two hundred up to me, I want to get cracking. I got opposition.' Any road, I sold they and said to Dougie, 'I want another hundred.'

He said, 'you'll never sell they.'

After a month I went and said, 'I want another thirty.'

'Eh,' he said.

I said, 'I want another thirty.'

So along come the fete and they used to give the person as sold the most tickets ten pound back, but it used to cost me double that to sell because when I went to someone's house they'd say, 'oh, I'm selling tickets too.' So you'd have to buy one off they too so I was out of pocket!

Anyway, at the fete they announced I was the winner.

Illustration 24: Wall hanging depicting Littleham Fete with John at the gate. Courtesy Littleham Tapissers.

Well in the meantime, Rene was complaining to me about her knee. She couldn't hardly walk on the other leg. Back to see Dr Ford again.

'Oh,' he said, 'I think you'd better go to Barnstaple again to see a specialist.' Specialist decided she wanted another operation. And this operation had to be done at Exeter. The time come, had to go to Exeter. So off I goes to Exeter. By this time I was retired from RGB. Up to Exeter every day for a fortnight to see my wife. And then they let her come home. And the leg never got no better, in fact it got worse, the operation wasn't no good. But she would insist she wanted to go out for a walk but she wouldn't have a wheelchair, which I was quite willing to push. So after dinner she'd catch hold of my arm and we'd walk up perhaps as far as the post office.

Then she'd say, 'I can't go no further,' and we'd go back. The next day we'd go as far as Mr Cook. Back home again.

Sitting home, she's not complaining about any of these things, never grumbles. So it went on a little way and I said, 'you seem to be catching hold of the furniture when you'm walking about.' So I looked at her and said, 'what's the trouble?'

She said, 'I can't see very well.' And by this time she was a diabetic, using the needle. Back to see Dr Ford again.

He said, 'you'll have to go to Barnstaple to see the eye specialist.' And they decided she'd got cataracts coming on her eyes and she'd have to have an operation but they couldn't do the two at once. Well, she come home and the sight was lovely in her one eye but she still had to go again for another operation. The time passed; a couple of months, back to Barnstaple, operation. Well then, she'd got so weak I had to walk upstairs behind her because I thought she'd fall back. So I said, 'how about having the single bed in the front room?'

'No,' she said, 'I'm not.'

So I seen Alan Smale. When he was little she used to take him and push him about in his pram. I said to him, 'would you come to my place and see if you can decide Aunty Rene to have a bed downstairs.'

'I will,' he said.

So after a week he come in and said, 'Aunty Rene, I think it's about time you had a bed downstairs.'

'No,' she said.

So us decided we was going to fetch the bed downstairs any road. So we put it in the front room. And that's where she had to sleep.

Well she got so bad I sent for Dr Ford and he said, 'well, John, it's getting bad not better. We live in hope. I think the time's come to have the nurse in everyday to wash her and dress her and that.'

Well, so it went on. We had her downstairs, the nurse coming in and she was still getting worse. I sent for Dr Ford again, he said, 'John, your wife should be in a home, you just cannot handle it.'

I said, 'would you repeat that again, doctor?'

He said, 'yes, your wife should be in a home and I can fix it up today.'

So I looked at my wife and thought, there's a promise I made to her years ago: whatever happens I'll look after you until you pass away. So I turned to Dr Ford and said, 'my wife's not going in a home, no way. I'll look after her.'

She was a wonderful person. She would never turn nobody away from the door and all her friends from the school used to come once a week, four or five of them and have a cup of tea and a biscuit. That's the finest thing ever happened to her really, the company.

Then one day I come down over the stairs and all the bedclothes was off her, she'd got no clothes on her, just laid on the bed and was in a proper mess. So I said to her, 'Rene, why have you been out of bed?'

'I haven't,' she said.

'You must have,' I said. 'The clothes is over there.' I knew she had; her mind was going. And she used to wet the bed. So a good friend of mine called Ann Gooding used to come to see her and she said, 'John, to save your mattress, I'll give you a proper sheet.'

The nurse come again. I said, 'my wife hasn't had a very good night.' I said, 'she's been sick all night.'

She said, 'have you saved it?'

I said, 'yes.' And in this sickness was lumps of stuff. So any road. It was cancer again, in the stomach.

The nurse said to me, 'I'll call back later but you send for Dr Ford.'

Sent for Dr Ford, he had one look at it and said she'd to go straight to Barnstaple again. So a lady that used to live over the road called Eileen a great friend, come with us in the car.

So off to Barnstaple, put her in the ward. Went on for a couple of days. By this time it was coming for Christmas and when I went away she said, 'if I'm not home for Christmas you put that little Christmas tree up that belonged to mother and father.'

Everything went on all right for a little while then I went up and all the curtains was closed. I thought they was bathing her. Rene didn't speak; she had a big mask on her face, trying to breath. I went out and said to the nurse, 'I want to see a doctor. I want to know what's going on about my wife.'

She said, 'you'll have to wait about half an hour because the doctor's going round the ward.'

I said, 'I'll wait.' So sure enough I did. The time come, it was a woman doctor. She sat me down. I said to her, 'Doctor, I want to know what's going on; they don't seem to be doing anything. Why haven't they operated?'

She said, 'we can't because your wife's heart is in a terrible state. I think it's a bad job.'

So off I come home again. Goes up and sees her again. Still the same, not speaking. Come home and I decided, it was on the nineteenth before Christmas, I thought to myself, I will put that tree up. We all live in hope. So I was half way through putting up the Christmas tree and the phone went. 'Are you Mr Devereux, nine Mount Pleasant?'

I said, 'yes, who's speaking?'

She said, 'are you sure? You are Mr Devereux?'

I said, 'yes, of course, I am.'

She said, 'your wife has just passed away.'

Oh dear, dear.

She said, 'you'll have to come straight away.'

So back to Alan Smale. I said, 'your Aunty Rene has just passed away and I got to get to Barnstaple and I don't want to go alone.'

He said, 'I'll take you up there.'

So off we got to Barnstaple again. Gets up there. Seen a nurse, then the doctor, then went in to see my wife. Come out from there. And the doctor said, 'I'd like to speak to you.'

I said, 'I want Alan to come as well.' They gave us a cup of tea and he explained that whatever had happened, there was no way they could save her. It was cancer all the time. So that put my mind to rest to think it was cancer that killed her.

I came back home. Eileen went home, she'd come with us to the hospital, and Alan stopped with me till the early hours of the morning. I said, 'go home.'

'I can't,' he said.

I said, 'I got to be on my own from now on.' So off he went home.

So who was we going to have for the funeral? I had a wonderful friend called Joan Swindler that used to live next door to me years ago. She was one of the loveliest people you could ever wish to have as a friend. And she used to come home and she would sit down and sort everything out for the funeral. She seen to everything for me. Phoned here, phoned everywhere. She worked hard.

The funeral come; Rene was cremated at Barnstaple.

Alan was bearer, Mr Brian Stevens and I forget who else. That's what she wished for. She had seven different things wrong with her, all at once.

We all come home to my house to have a cup of tea afterwards. All my good friends at Littleham seen to it. They laid the table, done everything. It was all right as long as people was there but after they went away Alan again said, 'John, I'm not going home.' And he stopped with me till one or half past in the morning and I said, 'you got to go.' So he went. I decided to sleep in the same bed as my wife was in. People said I couldn't do it but I did.

Different Times

So it went on. Now Alan, up to this day, will do anything for me. He works hard on the farm and he'll drop down tools on the farm and come home and do anything for me. But life was a bit of a struggle. I still done a little bit to the house to keep it up a little bit liveable.

Down the church I went cutting the grass for about 35 years, by hand. And Mr John Bromhead was in charge and Mervyn Cook and me, that was three, and Lionel Badcock, cut the grass. Job finished, the edges wanted trimming. So me and Derek Clarke that used to live down the rectory, we volunteered to cut the edges, all by hand. And I still do a few little graves down there today. So any road, Mr Bromhead come to see me and said we want the main water put down to the church. So I said, that's quite all right, I'm free to give you a hand. So we started off with a small digger, a little one, in the churchyard, and over by the porch. We went right across the churchyard with that small one, through the hedge, then we had to get a bigger one. And from there we dug up across the green right alongside Mr Brian Steven's field, until we got to John Bromhead's property. And every day when it come one o'clock, I'd say 'I've got to get home for my dinner.'

John said, you're not going home, you're coming up to dinner with me and Doris.'

After four days or so, time comes to lay the pipe in. So right by the tap in the corner, over the field, got half way and we run out of pipe. So John had to go and get another length. Any road, John comes back, fixes it up, joins it up and we get up to where the water board people are by the old school. The next job is to get hold of the water board to come and connect up. So I said to John, after a couple of days when they could come along, 'would it be a good idea to turn the water on to see if they joints are okay?' So they turned the water on slow. After half an hour he was all right; he wasn't leaking. With the bulldozer, filled it all in, right the way down. So after that, job finished. A good job done. They can use the fresh water now for making tea in the church.

Illustration 26: St Swithun's Church and the old Rectory

So any road. Claude Nicholls, the man that does all the bell-ringing and all the good work in the churchyard at the present moment, decided that we should have toilets down there; a portable toilet. We decided that we'd get a digger and dig out a place in the bank where they two old cottages used to be years ago in the car park.

Cut it out. Proper job. So along comes the portable toilet. Fixed him in and they dug out a fair bit too much so we had to put a wall

all round, what they called dry walling. So me and John Bromhead and Claude Nicholls done the job.

So any road, that was that.

Then the path people in Exeter, who looked after all the paths around, decide the path across Mr Brian Steven's field should be altered because it used to go along the top of the cemetery and in the back land going down the back of the church. So we had a big meeting and they wanted to come through the hedge and down across the churchyard which was very steep and down by the graves. Any road, at the meeting – there was a lot of people there – we beat them to it. We stopped them doing it.

So after a while, everything seemed to be gone and done, I walked down to the churchyard one morning. And sure enough there's John Bromhead starting to dig a hole outside the gates. I said, 'Hello John. What's up?'

He said, 'the drain is broken.'

So we dug it out by hand. *(Ed. John was in his late eighties at this point)* Got down and sure enough, yes, the drain was broke. We decide then we want some cement so off I go to RGB and got the cement. Back to John Bromhead's, where he'd got a mixer, and mixed up a couple of wheelbarrow's full. And we got a piece of pipe off Mr Smith from down the Rectory and cemented this pipe all round about a foot deep. Any road, we decide then we'd get some water and put in the drains up by the porch. Sure enough, it trickled out in to his pool. So me and John had to fill it in. Clean it up and the job is done.

Anyway, it's all coming to an end now. I think I done enough for the church and the village hall. I'm still living there now, still hanging on through all those nine years since Rene's been gone. I'm ninety-two now, born on the 21st October 1915. The eldest that's left of the family.

I lost my two sisters within two months of each other. A few years back my youngest sister, Joyce, died at Cleehonger, that was with cancer, and after that, a few weeks after, my older sister, Lena, died – with cancer again. So I think I'm a lucky man to have escaped it all. There's only two of us left now, me the oldest and Donny, the youngest brother.

So any road, when Rene was still alive we picked up another friend which was called Pam. And she come to live down the road in a new house with her son. Now I'd never knowed this lady before in my life. So any road. I used to do a bit of grass-cutting to make ends meet, and I used to cut the grass for her. So this went on and then she picked up with Dave Hogan, a man which was a professional at his job up at the college. And I never met in all my life a better couple living. They was so helpful and kind to me and they still are to this day.

So how'm I going to thank them? Well, he lived at Landkey. He sold his house, Pam sold her house and they bought a piece of ground belonging to Mr Alvis down Church Lane; they'm going to have a house built. So any road. It went through and I decided to myself then, whatever that man wants me to do to the building of that house I'll do. I was retired. And I used to go down there and watch the diggers. Before that there was a big fowl house to be taken down. So Dave and me had to take the roof off. Weekends, worked hard. And before that I spent hours down there on my own in the daytime.

And he'd come home and say, 'John, I've got to pay you for the work you've done.'

I turned round and said, 'Dave, whatever I do to the house, you're not to pay me a penny because you and your wife already paid me in kindness.'

So after a while the house got built and after that they'd invite me down sometimes on Sunday to dinner. All sit down round the table and I was treated as if I was one of their own. So any road, time goes on, Dave said to me one day, 'John,' he said, 'when you was in the army what did you serve in?'

I said, 'the Royal Engineers.'

He said, 'where's your medals?'

I said, 'I didn't apply for them.'

And he said, 'I think you deserve some because you was in bomb disposal up in London for two and a half years, digging up bombs.'

So he decided he'd find out where you got medals from and I think they come from an army place at Gloucester. Sure enough, he got me two lovely medals after a couple of months. But he wasn't satisfied so he gets hold of Chatham barracks and explains what had happened to me. One thing and another and I got a certificate now in a photograph right in front of me, thanking me for my services, in bomb disposal. It come on my birthday.

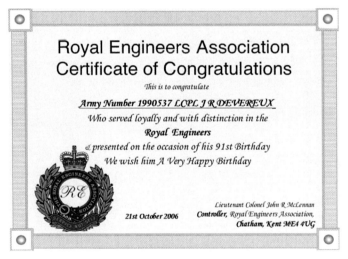

Illustration 27: John's certificate from his regiment of which he was so proud

Dave said to me before that, 'John,' he said, 'I'm going to Chatham. I'd like you to come along.'

I thought Chatham? What the devil do he want me to go to Chatham for? I said, 'I got a bad leg, I can't stick the walking about.'

He said, 'you don't have to.'

So he asked me again and I said no and I wished I'd said yes, cause he never told me I was going to get this certificate, to present to me there. Then my birthday come and sure enough out come this certificate and I was never so thrilled in my life that that man had gone to all that trouble just to get that through for me.

Illustration 28: John with his pilot after his first ever flight –
a visit to the Isles of Scilly on his 91st Birthday

So now I'm living on my own in the same little cottage. To me it's my home; to other people it's an old broken down house. Any road, I've lived here so long I've got used to it. And I sit here at night going back through my life since I was a little child; the hard times I had, going to school with a bit of bread and jam wrapped up in newspaper and shoved in my pocket, me and my sister, and we'd go to the tap in the corner for water. And it never got no better.

All those years have passed and I'm sorry to say a few months ago I lost a dear old friend of mine, Lionel Badcock, that lived in the village in Culver Cottage with his sister Aileen. And he'd lived there all his life. Seventy-seven, and he died, sudden.

Earlier on, he said to me one day, 'Why don't you drive to the traction engine club at Chapleton?'

(Ed. Lionel, along with several other Littleham men, was a keen vintage machinery enthusiast. John obtained an old engine driven water pump and regularly exhibited it at rallies.)

Illustration 29: Lionel & John in unusual attire! – Picture from John's effects

And me and him was always together. And in the end we was the only two together with the stationary engine. The others had all moved on. And after he died I decided I'd give up the stationary engine and I haven't been since. It was a very sad job when he died – up top of his garden one Sunday afternoon.

Any road, I'm still clogging along. And I don't like Christmas because it brings back memories to me about my wife – she lay dead over the Christmas – and I'm sorry to say that I'm very lonely at times. Then all of a sudden Pam or Dave will come up or I'll go to see them, then that cheers me up again, it's just like winding a clock up.

And after ninety-two years, I think I've told you the story. And I only hope the younger people today will understand what we people went through years ago. I give seven years of my life to save people so they could live in peace. But I don't think they understand; they're not old enough. It hasn't happened to they. I hope it don't.

So now I've come to the end of my story. And great thanks to all my friends for where I am today. And I only hope we'll go on being friends. Which I couldn't ask for anything better in my life.

Thank you one and all.

The story have ended.

Illustration 30: The war memorial in Littleham Churchyard

Last Things

Johnny, as he affectionately became known, died on 29th February 2008 after a trying illness. His funeral service was held at St Swithun's, Littleham. David Hogan delivered the following Eulogy.

John Richard Devereux
21st October 1915 – 29 February 2008

Eulogy

If you knew a cantankerous man from Littleham who would argue that black was white, then you probably are *acquainted* with John Devereux.

If you were to meet a red car travelling to, or from, Littleham driven by a man who steadfastly refused to reverse to enable you to pass, then you have probably *passed* John Devereux.

If you dared to question the trump rule whilst playing cards and suffered the indignity of a robust reprimand then you were probably *at a table* with John Devereux.

If you had the temerity to challenge a young soldier from Hereford, at Top Camp at Westward Ho! during the Second World War then you most likely will have been *knocked out* by a fist belonging to John Devereux.

If you were to park your car opposite no. 9 Mount Pleasant then John Devereux would very soon become *acquainted* with you.

If we found a salesman selling raffle tickets for the fete at our door then we will have been persuaded to part with our money by John Devereux. (It is probably true that there will have been very few raffles in Littleham during the last years where the tickets, if not sold by, have been *torn and folded* by John Devereux.)

If any of these attributes reflect your recollections of a Littleham man, then you have almost certainly been *acquainted* with John Devereux.

--0--

The 20th Century Jewish Philosopher, Martin Buber, spent much of his life considering the relationship that exists between people.

He identified that most relationships between people are on the level that is reflected in these observations about John.

However, Buber went on to consider a more deep and spiritual connection that was possible between people. He called it the "I-Thou" relation.

He believed that the "I-Thou" relation leads to a freedom of interaction, unity and understanding enabling a free exchange of experience and ideas.

He considered that in the "I-Thou" relationship, human beings do not perceive each other as consisting of specific, isolated qualities, but engage in a dialogue involving each other's whole being.

I believe that I was fortunate enough to have such a connection with John. Perhaps others did too.

This connection, this friendship, demonstrated that behind the practical exterior of the person there was a deep thinking, sensitive individual.

Knowing this may change our perspective on the man whom we mourn today.

The way John appeared to the world was moulded by a life hard as it was eventful.

Nevertheless, behind the tough exterior was a loving, sensitive man who, quietly and anonymously expressed the fundamental tenets of his Christian faith in his daily life.

Because of this anonymity, itself a Christian quality, I suspect few were aware of his quiet consideration and unspoken care for others irrespective of their class or creed, so often expressed in unseen acts of kindness and consideration.

His charity was indeed a private but very real expression.

Perhaps his most often heard expression when he was considering life and his experience of it was "…what's it all about?"

It may seem strange to us who knew him on a day to day basis to appreciate that he did often consider, very seriously, the imponderable questions that persistently confront us all about existence.

He often talked about, but never understood, inequality and the contrariness of people's attitudes. Disingenuousness in the actions and attitudes of others would invoke great sadness. Whilst he could be relied upon to be uncomfortably even–handed and genuine with everyone he had dealings with, sadly, he had a deeply ingrained awareness of his assumed, lowly station in life which seemed to doggedly hold him back.

John came to be part of our family and was a regular and enthusiastic member at family gatherings.

We share with John's own family a great sense of loss at his death. We are all very thankful that, to use Buber's expression, "we came alongside John Devereux".

Our lives are, indeed, richer for his friendship.

--0--

If we had known a child who slept in a room without windows with just a sack to keep out the weather, then we would have *known* the boy John Devereux.

If we had known a boy whose father defended his mother against the assault of his employer and as a consequence was cast out of their tied cottage then we would have *known* the youth John Devereux.

If we had known a young man whose mother lost her mind following the assault and subsequent eviction then we would have *known* the man John Devereux.

If we had known a young private who was light on his feet in his company football team and good with his fists in the company boxing ring then we would have *known* the soldier John Devereux.

If we lived at Twyford Avenue in Shepherd's Bush, London during the Second World War then our lives may well have been *saved* by Lance Corporal J.R.Devereux of the Bomb Disposal Squad of The Royal Engineers Regiment. (Indeed there are many in London, who are unaware that they owe their lives to John Devereux as a result of this most dangerous of activities).

If we had known of John's grief at the unfaithfulness of his first wife and his trauma at the subsequent divorce whilst he risked his life in London in the army, then we would have been *very close* to John Devereux.

If we had supported Appledore or Bideford football clubs in the middle of the 20th Century then we would have certainly *watched* the talents of a youthful footballer, John Devereux.

If we knew of his love, so often stated recently, for his beloved wife Rene then we will have *known* John Devereux.

If we were fed by Aunty Rene in her capacity as dinner lady, as many here will have been, then, not only will we have grown strong and healthy as a result, but we will also have *known* Uncle John Devereux, her husband.

If you found yourself in need of labour or the help of a strong arm then you most probably *asked* John Devereux.

If you needed a delivery of animal feed, fertiliser, building materials, or bread then it was probably *carried* in by "Driver" John Devereux.

If you discovered that a church gate had been painted, a new stonewall constructed, a drain cleared or hedges and verges cut in Littleham then you have probably *seen* the work of John Devereux.

If you found a bag of runner beans, bucket of onions or a bouquet of sweet peas on your doorstep, then it was likely a *gift* from an anonymous John Devereux.

If your village street football squad included an octogenarian in its line up, then you're under 16 and had John Devereux on your side.

If you needed to know where anyone or anything was in Littleham then you would most likely have *asked* John Devereux.

Indeed, if you knew anything of note about Littleham and its people then you probably *learned* it from John Devereux.

--0--

It is tempting to say that he leaves behind him a void, difficult to fill. I believe that the opposite is the reality.

He leaves behind a legacy. His life, apart from being an example of personal and physical strength, reflects rectitude, courage in adversity, determination, uncomfortable directness, unconditional love, affection, charity and forgiveness.

Good Bye Old Soldier – your watch is over – your Duty has been done.

David M Hogan
March 2008

Illustration 31: John's last resting place in the Church Yard of St Swithun's, Littleham, North Devon, United Kingdom. It can be found beneath the copper beech tree amongst the graves of many of his friends. The memorial stone has as its central feature, an engraving of the emblem of the Royal Engineers with whom John served for seven years of his life.

Acknowledgements:

Illustration 1 –Ballingham Station –photo courtesy of Tim Ward – www.wyevalleyhistory.net

Illustration 2 –Dewchurch School –Picture courtesy of www.herefordshiretrail.com

Illustration 3 –Muck cart image –photo courtesy of www.thompsontrading.co.uk/

Illustration 4 –Blowing the organ –picture courtesy of David Banga –www.pbase.com/banga/

Illustration 5 –The outside toilet –picture courtesy of tre.ngfl.gov uk

Illustration 6 –Timber carriage –picture courtesy of www.southlakes-uk.co.uk

Illustration 7 –Milk Maids –photo courtesy of www3.shropshire-cc.gov.uk

Illustration 8 –Milk Churns –image courtesy of www.igg.org.uk

Illustration 9 –Threshing machine –photo courtesy of las.new-england.net.au

Illustration 10 –Lance Corporal Devereux J.R.–photo from John's effects

Illustration 11 –The little brown case "I carried me football boots to war in." – photo courtesy of David Hogan.

Illustration 12 –Pillbox –June 1940. Picture courtesy of the BBC.

Illustration 13 –Bomb Disposal –early 1940's. Picture courtesy of Lt Col E.E. Wakeling ERD

Illustration 14 –Aerial view of Top Camp, Westward Ho! – photo courtesy of Westward Ho! History

Illustration 15 –Top Camp Courtyard, 1939 – photo courtesy of Westward Ho! History

Pamela Vass

Pamela is a Devon author who finds inspiration in the people and places of the West Country. Her writing includes *Seeds of Doubt*, a novel set against the backdrop of rumours of Government interference with the weather at the time of the 1952 Lynmouth floods, and *Shadow Child*, a novel following the fortunes of a young boy determined to solve the mystery of his mother's disappearance.

She often includes extensive historical research in her books, particularly in her most recent publication, *The Power of Three*, the story of Devon inventor Thomas Fowler. She has given numerous presentations of her findings, most notably to the Computer Conservation Society at the Science Museum in May 2005. For further information on Fowler see www.mortati.com/glusker

For more on Pamela see www.boundstonebooks.co.uk

David Hogan

David is primarily an educationalist and computer scientist. He has lectured in computer science and associated subjects for over 30 years. In 2000 he became a laureate of the Smithsonian Institute in Washington DC USA following his seminal work on video conferencing to aid the geographically disadvantaged student. This work is published in the Smithsonian archives and in the UK at the British Library. Papers by David Hogan have also been published by the British Educational Communications & Technology Agency (BECTA.). David was also invited by the United Kingdom Education Research Network Authority (UKERNA) to assist with a pilot study into quality of service protocols within the Joint Academic Network of the UK (JANET). He is a member of the Joint Information Systems Council of the United Kingdom where he advises on the development of the UK academic network (JANET)